KU-591-571

Burned   All My Witches

an autobiography in verse

Liam O' Meara

RIPOSTE BOOKS DUBLIN

First Published in 2001
RIPOSTE BOOKS
28 Emmet Rd., Dublin 8. Ireland

ISBN: 1901596060

© Liam O' Meara 2001
Printed by Docuprint Dublin

ALL RIGHTS RESERVED

Limited edition 500 copies

When the heart weeps
for what it has lost
the spirit laughs
for what it has found*

*anonymous Sufi aphorism

Acknowledgements

Poems in this book have appeared in *The Sunday Tribune, The Limerick Leader, Poetry Ireland Review, Riposte, The Ingredients of Poetry, Litspeak (Germany), Inchicore and Kilmainham Heritage Journal,* and *Golden Echoes-* an anthology of winning entries to the Gerard Manley Hopkins Competition.

I would like to especially thank those few who were first to be exposed to my poetry over the years: Liam Kelly, who from our school days was first to give sound critical analysis and practical advise; Eithne Hogan- a kindred spirit; and Michael O'Flanagan, with whom I have collaborated on numerous literary projects in recent years. My thanks also, to the various members, past and present, of the Syllables Writers' Group; members and supporters of The Inchicore Ledwidge Society; Sean Carey and contributors to the Dublin Poetry Conference. Finally, those of my associates in the broader field of poetry who were always there when needed: Eileen Casey, Christine Broe, Áine Miller, Elaine Murphy, Denis Collins, Ann Comerford, Maeve O'Sullivan, Michael Herron, Marian Finan, James Conway, Marian J. Murphy, and many others.

Photographs
Cover: Winetavern Street, showing the huckster shops; frontispiece- Winetavern Street, courtesy of Peter Pearson, the late Malachy Hynes and the O'Brien Press. Thanks also, to Darren Keogh for artistic computer enhancement of some of the photos; Damien Maddock and DM Prints; artist, writer, historian Pat Liddy and The Irish Times for drawing of the Brazen Head; The Searcher magazine for photo of the slave collar.

ned ai͏   ᴺᴼ Liam O'Meara

Contents

7

Three

<u>With My Wife And Children In Inchicore</u>

Four

<u>Loss Of My Parents</u>

Five

Reflections

9

Foreword

I was born on Ussher's Quay in the heart of Dublin, in rooms overlooking the river Liffey at the front, and at the back overlooking the courtyard of The Brazen Head, Dublin's oldest Inn. My parents were rich in virtues that no money could ever buy: ours was a happy home. One morning, a removal van heralded our exodus to a foreign place. The van arrived earlier than expected and there was no time for me to change out of my night-shirt. The family piled into the open backed van already containing our furniture. It was a rocky ride to Ballyfermot. I was left holding a goldfish (still in the bowl). I have always had the feeling that I left something behind.

Following my marriage, some thirty years later, I moved with my wife to Inchicore where I have lived for the past twelve years. Here, I can never cross the square of St. Michael's Estate without being aware of its past history: Richmond Barracks, where Francis Ledwidge trained as a soldier; where a total of 3,000 people were detained following the Easter rising; and where the leaders of the Rising were court-martialled prior to their execution. The gymnasium is today preserved as a shrine to these men.

This book is about learning to live with loss: the vacuum left in the wake of childhood mysteries solved - the fading of innocent illusions, the changing face of Dublin city, and the passing of my parents. Children, without knowing it, occupy a world of poetry where they daily encounter some new object of mystery and beauty, which they then thoroughly examine for the first time. Poets often attempt to gain re-entry to this world. My 'witches' were but harmless women: one, physically impaired by polio- all too prevalent at that time - another, a hardworking shop assistant, while yet another was a widow dressed habitually in Victorian black lace and beads. The latter was Mary Ryan. She owned most of the properties in the Ussher's Quay area, including the shop on the ground floor of where we lived - The Creamery, or Dairy as it was known locally.

Understandably, death must play a significant part in any treatise on the subject of loss. Chapter four is devoted to my late parents. My fond memories of them continue to sustain me.

Liam O'Meara

1

Early days on Ussher's Quay

CASTLECON...
BR...

Desert Cowboy
(The Creamery, 4, Ussher's Quay)

Tinkle, tinkle bell
the closing of the door

departure

left me on a compromise
and a wild pledge.

The butter-box
was a lame mule
unable to carry dreams
my tears had a taste of salt.

On foot across barren boards
my progress slight
although the room
-the shop- was small.

Miss Hayden paused
-light catching the cheek-
her stainless blade
raised above tobacco
she glared

This knife, (some say

without a wipe)
      cut butter from the slab
made icecream into wafers
                      sliced
the ham, the cheese
         ready for the scales
on Fridays, lopped the heads
from fresh open-mouthed fish.

At my regained quarter
              I resolved:
butter-box
        on top of butter-box
made a reasonable horse

          and Mammy?

     Tinkle tinkle bell
the opening the door

Mammy- shopping bags full-
would come galloping home.

Timepiece

in my time
it was the piano in the Liffey
and for years after its departure
people would still speak with fondness
when a memory was stirred

of local scamps
who used to climb on board
in spite of the muck and stench;
and many a tale was related,
many a wedding or a birth,
- the very act of conception dated
to certain nights
when the wind could be heard
sing against its cords.

Lord ! what would they have thought
of a clock in the Liffey,
a gigantic live clock
alternating with the water level
always a foot below the surface.

But those city folk were scattered
to the wilds beyond the city
to the mudlands of emerging towns
the forests of tv aerials

the gaunt white of corporation schemes;

and the cobble stones familiar once
on the streets along the quays
now pave the yuppie wonderland
of Temple Bar.

The clock to hail the new millennium
ran out of time:
long before the appointed date
and the ballyhoo of fireworks
barely left the skies
its mass of slime and poison quills
was hauled from view -
the piano had lasted longer.

Yet, you'll see the tourists
stooped across the bridge, scanning
whiffy waters for that emerald jewel,

while at the drop-in centre further on
there's some old down-an'-out
trying to gleen the magic numbers
                    of the National Lotto.

Envoy

"aaah,
the Liffey clock,
the Liffey Clock

ya can say
what ya may

but ya can't say
that a Dub
wouldn't give ya
the time a day

it's fourteen zillion
seconds
ti the next
Millennium

an it's 10
for the price
of 8

work it out
yourself son"

Mrs. Fury was a local music teacher who gave piano lessons. Many remember her instruction aids: *"Here comes Felix walking* and *"Little brown jug."* She wore black clothes with a net over her head. It was she who owned the piano. Apparently, she noticed that it had woodworm and paid a man by the name of Curtis to dump it. He choose the nearest available spot- the Liffey, just yards from where she conducted her business.

A Flight Of Stairs

following the fall
an icepop placed on my eyebrow
told the pain would soon depart
and left to heal

seated on the bottom step
I finished off the icepop
sure enough

the pain ascended

Dedicated to my sister, Joan (Sr. Mary Ann Joseph) who was the good
Samaritan with the ice-pop.   She left home shortly after this, aged
fifteen , to join the Sisters of Mercy in Midhurst, Sussex.

Woolworth's Of Thomas Street

Sweetmeats of all sorts
gave a certain scent
no youngster would forget

and it was the place
for ice-cream, model airplanes
marbles, books, toy soldiers

parents remembered it
as 'The Sixpenny Store'
where "everything was sixpence"

you had a sister
a relation, or you knew someone
who worked there

one of its many outlets
today a link

in a different chain
doors kept open, flanked
by pedlars of the 'Samson' weed

the soft centre of happy thought
confounded by the glum faces

of the unemployed

a human tapeworm stretching
growing, as the payclerk adds
to the paper cone
                -measures the coin

no sixpenny pieces these days
regular, or crooked

The former Woolworth's store is today used as a Social Welfare office.

Burned   All My Witches

They were easier to spot in those days
        - the woman in the shop at Winetavern Street
where we used to buy our sweets when we were kids
- *she* was a witch

the harness on her leg it was, gave her away

I, pretending to be shy, would linger in the doorway
while my big sister did the business,
                    parting with our pennies
before turning towards me- the hand already tucked
inside a white paper bag

                    it did not end there
for often I was nearly poisoned,
                by the placement of liquorice
among the sweets: recognising instantly the foul taste
I would give them to my sister, who was immune
and seemed to like them

Today, the huckster shop, that whole row of shops
has vanished; and it's as though I imagined it
        together with the witch on her stick of liquorice
arriving at the counter   just   in   time ....

How I miss that woman and that shop and that street.

Floorboards And A Stray Cat

pored over porridge
         oatmeal vapours steaming
my eyelids open

who were these men
taking all our furniture?

in my night-shirt
         in the back of the gaping van
my job- holding the goldfish bowl

me and Goldie
swashing about on the high seas

father's voice faltering :
         "Bally-far-out...a house
...imagine...after fourteen years"

watching the past drift
a blizzard of road

what sort of place was this?
         no footpaths
miles of mud

the church
and spattered corrugated hoardings

a forest of TV aerials
fields...   a roundabout....   more houses
the van slowing down

a giant sycamore looming to the front
the family pulling up

2

Growing up in Ballyfermot

Icon in the Church of the Assumption Ballyfermot

The Family

The woman broomed the shavings
from the sunlit floor
as her husband busily
chiselled out some more

each one an eye
for the task that was before them
and one eye for the little boy
who stood between them

no sound of brushing besom
or thud against wood
only the situation spoke
from how the three stood

no movements, no words used
or pretence to describe
the wonder of their thinking
yet the scene survived

and lived, lived in the minds
of children as we sat
encompassed by the preacher
giving his wordy chat

the sunlight breaking
the mid-morning crust
the fixed stare of the little boy
through the shavings, through the dust.

My first poem, written when I was eighteen, recalling when I was six.

To My Best Friend

dedicated to Deirdre O'Brien

I liked the fact that you liked me
and I liked you
for that
and for no particular reason
except perhaps your fuzzy hair
like a ginny-jo, but brown

together we'd sit on the carpet
in your mother's house
playing at tea parties or school -
you the teacher
I the pupil- after all
you were seven, I was only six

you told me about your Holy Communion -
of the money you had collected -
you showed me your long white dress
worn only once

and one day when you were not there
I saw men carrying a white box
people said that you were dead
struck by a car while playing piggy-beds
-the girls game

then I heard how the 'piggy' left the path
how you'd stretched to fetch it
when the car had come up
hugging the kerb

my childhood joys were held that day
trapped between the squares
you 'd mapped in chalk

it was a time to believe
my shadow and I
swapped places
needing to be with you

and that shadow today
when flesh
becomes the poet

I never knew why my mother used to take me to the O' Brien house or
how she came to know Mrs O'Brien (Patty Madden). Thirty nine years
later, I was one day contacted by Brendan O'Brien, who had seen an
article about my research on poet Francis Ledwidge. I visited his home
in Springfield, Tallaght, and as he was showing newspaper items and
explaining to me that he was a descendent of the Mc Goona's of Meath,
my eye caught a photograph of Ussher's Quay hanging on the wall. It
emerged that our families had lived side by side on the Quays. Both
families were re-housed in Ballyfermot. Brendan, next amazed me by
telling me how his mother left Ballyfermot after his baby sister had been
tragically killed following her first Holy Communion. I knew at once he
was speaking of my friend Deirdre.
Obviously, my mother on meeting a familiar face from the Quays began
visiting the O'Briens at their new home and that was how I got to know
Deirdre. How bizarre, to find that my little friend was a direct
descendent of Matty Mc Goona, best friend of Francis Ledwidge.

Stages

the talking point that morning
-the Americans on the moon

buoyed by Man's achievement
we went through the motions
of that 'Giant Leap'
taking off the astronauts
while we waited

and waited

and waited

and waited

and waited

and waited

and waited

the 78A rattled past
black full, puffing fumes

late for school
we landed
in trouble
with the Nuns

Lesson In Blue

the air was blue the morning after
I had stayed awake long past my bed
writing an essay for school
and had used a razor blade to shave
a point upon my pencil
and had then replaced the blade where I found it
back in father's razor
so that he *would not* be upset

I remember him that morning
cheerfully en route to the bathroom,
"I think I'll give myself a scrape"

Moving Statues

Not the Virgin Mary
but the halo of Saint Joseph
moved from its spot
in the church at Ballyfermot.
It was after the priest

told the congregation
that the halo was made of gold.
That night it moved
flitted about the moonlit church
and it was seen no more.

Identity

Who would expect to find a perfect statue in Ballyfermot?

Somebody did.

       Ballyfermot, where the faceless
Virgin Mary is recognisable to all,

               but to no-one
more than the man who defaced her;

              whose name
serves no mention,
       whose hammer speaks his creed;

and who forever will remain unrecognised,

like a headstone shattered
          like a statue unknown.

His Suit Of Armour

.... the lash of a three inch buckle belt
across a wooden head-board after midnight;
frantic untying of laces and the drop

from knee height of an 'army' boot; rustle
of newspaper casings being pulled from
underneath his trouser legs; thud of corduroys

upon the oilcloth and the boards; the near
to breaking of the springs taking all
of fourteen stone; sighs, relief moans

as the 'peels' were drawn, - sleeve of a topcoat
tucked around his neck, (feet having found
the heated iron in the towel); and then,   the lull

the lull

before the train, you know - before the snoring
would begin

The iron in question was a solid iron, made from a melted down railway
track, as indeed, were other items in the house, such as the frying pan
and the cobbler's last. My father's leather belt with brass buckle, also
came from 'The Works', as did many a strap and holster set for his
aspiring young cowboys. These were favours from fellow C.I.E
employees who knew where to go if they ever needed glass cut for a
picture frame. Some, did not know his name, but everyone knew 'The
Glazier.'   I have an abiding memory of my father, prone to
uncontrollable bouts of sneezing , who had one night retrieved the iron
from the bed in order to heat it; as he was about to descend the stairs, he
let go of the iron and down the stairs it went. We thought the end of the
world had arrived.

Inchicore Works

Through the "Khyber Pass"
twice a day
for forty years
my father walked,
his cap and forehead
always a few
inches
above the rest.
In the narrowness
of the lane
looking orderly,
obedient
and though weary on return
finding extra pace
to take him home;
earful of foreman,
mindful of shop steward,
lungs full of paint;
perhaps just looking forward to another argument
              - more crossfire- in the morning
with the 'Free-Stater' opposite

A brief pause for the Irish Press
and a woman he could never pass
"Mother Ireland" at the corner.

Then, with paper rolled up in voluminous pocket
- arms free to his stride - he would take home
'the recipe' for our *'frugal comfort'*.

The 'Khyber Pass'

Inchicore Works- previous page

'Khyber Pass': colloquial name for the workers entrance to C.I.E. railway works. *"The recipe for frugal comfort,"* is a quote from a speech by President Eamonn De Valera . 'The Free Stater opposite,' refers to workmate, Joe Kelly who worked for most of his life across the bench from my father in the carriage shop. They were on different sides of the political divide: the Civil War was relived on a daily basis in the works. Sworn enemies as they were, nevertheless a peculiar sort of bond was formed and it was always Joe who took home my father's wages whenever he was sick. By strange coincidence, I met and befriended Joe's son, Liam, in college. We've been friends for over thirty years, almost as long as our parents worked and argued side by side.

Father's Watch

I once found and wound
my father's watch
wound it tight
there was a whirring sound
as hands flew round and round
then stopped

if I hadn't been so little
he'd have "taken his belt"

father's hands were huge
and if they struck would hurt
his face said it all

Quartz followed next
disposable watches, LCD
and aeroplane pilot time

I last found my father
20 minutes late
his body wound tight
his spirit flown
to some other place
beyond the blue drapes
the sound of nurses moving
round and round
a candle on a locker
burning

Neighbours

We shared a canopy
the first number of strokes
before taking on the hazards
of respective ladders

I was putting brown
over cream emulsion paint
while Freddie next door
pocketing a rag passed through the window
                              by his miss's
put cream- the same shade of cream
                              over brown

We stopped a moment
- dipped brushes

I remember Freddie's face
and I'm sure he remembers mine.

Hats And Tails

a rat would need a top hat
before it could enter Freddie's garden
rats were my problem
as though they belonged to me
"If they get into your attic..."

I wondered if that night
when he stood up
from his ménage of flowers
rats would discriminate his place from mine

as he spoke I crouched
on my hands and knees
digging out my weeds

but I was planning for this moment
waiting for the chance
when he would leave his door ajar
and I would scurry up his stairs
ravage all his wires....

41

26 Croftwood Drive

at times putting in the key
I would remember the first time
when I found it was the right one
the lock turned easily 'round
and the heavy door fell open

our first house, our new home
and how happy we were

but now I think on how things change
as for the last time I slam this door shut
but wait

I must have left my watch inside
ticking my life away unsupervised

now, where's that key again

3

With my wife and children in Inchicore

St. Michael's C.B.S. National School Inchicore, comprising of the recreation rooms and infamous gymnasium of the old Richmond Barracks. Unit three was used recently in the filming of 'Angela's Ashes'.

The Occasional Croak And Chirp

4.40am. and Paradise
multitudinous chirping of birds
- that I would pull back the veil
to gaze
at this Garden of Eden

but I know as I lie here -
the third floor -
behind that curtain
is a graveyard

5.45, the cry of a child
and the thump
of awakened parents
a work weary sleep robbed father pleads
"In the name of Jesus"

while in the graveyard
life continues

with the occasional croak and chirp

Where I Live

"Gik-nah," explained son to younger sister
freeing the bird
watching it fly, whoosh up away around then
 down
back to the street below

"They contaminate the loft"

well at least he didn't beat out its brains:
you can see the bloodied smear on balcony walls
where the so called pigeon fanciers settle
                              unwelcome squatters

              by the neck
I pour my harvest collar
seeing it bubble froth and rise to meet
as on this stool I perch among the 'racers'
in this haunt, not my haunt
wondering, should I join in the babble
                              or risk exposure

'Giknah': colloquial name for a common street pigeon.

The Marble Arch
(Public House, Inchicore)

Swans touching down
on liquid runway

red
to flickering orange
green
traffic flows

a vain bird, sunrinsed
in ripples of concentric peach

I cross the footbridge
catch the bleeps
wade between the built up banks
reach
the only telephone around
unspoilt

Fitzgerald's Marble Arch
through perspex looms
carpet eking from the lounge

There I will sit (will sip)
and brood
give flight to agile thoughts
- that they may one day earn
crusty approval.

Dying In Mc Dowell's

same backs and bottoms
 on the same bar stools
'The Stetson' as usual,
heading the cast:

> *"it's a snipe"*
> *"a woodcrest"*
> *"a woodcock"* - the brylcreamed one
> *"a blackcock, surely?"*

> *"it's 50p"*- Mrs Ward, re-adjusting her glasses
> shuffling on to more serious stuff-
> > *"now Liam, the usual?"*

    I'm old here, at one with the place
drab creams, browns, abandoned snug
and the footworn rawboards
               receiving my last
ash to ashes cigarette leaving
a near perfect John Player King Size
               ('Blues') box
exuding essence:
               Virginia on silvergilt
tissue of white lies lining
cellophane varnished cardboard
               (all I'm covered for)
and next I notice The Government

                    in horizontal pose
tax happy tongue in cheek
                    remembering
to mention (to whisper you might say)
for those who read small print
                    through mist,
the slightly pissed
through rising haze of nicotine
                    (I squint)

   smokers   die   *younger*

'The Stetson': the late Johnny O'Reilly, local butcher and well known Inchicore character. He was seldom seen without his stetson hat and as he was a frequenter of Mc Dowells, this may partly be the reason why the pub was known colloquially at one time as 'The High Chaparral.' Johnny bred his own sheep and they used to graze on the land behind his butcher shop- a most unusual sight in an urban area. Other great characters of Mc Dowell's, no longer with us, include Harry Boland and former president of I.C.T.U, Matt Merrigan.

Goldenbridge

on the lawn seagulls nod and look
but in no great hurry:
they have the pitch and soon they'll leave
when schoolgirls come with jogging knees
in soft blue skirts on throbbing earth
up to the old facade and on
to modern rooms beyond.

I never walk that far, but turn
as if from forbidden ground
down to my left, to the nursery
with my seedling clinging.

The ash, that has just got out of bed
- bird adorned, no leaves;
the evergreen, confounding time;
the proud poplars in beards

A secret way, a gap in the yew,
three-legged along the path by the wall;
we climb the steps, breath after breath,
            arrive.
The grey nun smirks.
Each day I kiss my little girl goodbye

Dawn

sunlight
        scavenging rooks
silhouette of towers
    white 'tea-stained' facades
graffito notoriety
          but peace

that can be broken
  by the revving rape of engine
or shattering of glass
  or scuff of boots on concrete
when hooded youths scramble
          dart
but peace

turns to disquiet
synapses trigger
and a thought penetrates -

crime thrives on complacency

A Tale Of Two Santas

her new 'fella' fell.... up the stairs
in the small hours of Christmas
carrying parcels of good things
for his adopted kids

and there on the balcony
straight from the pub
carrying parcels of good things
was the old 'fella' and father
of most of the children

it was oh oh oooh !
as a big 'mill' began
sending toys skyward and down
with herself in the doorway
pleading peace "*You'll kill yourselves*"
"*You'll wake the kids*"
"*You'll let Santa's secret out*"

but Santa one had Santa two
by a hold of the short and curly
while the other tried to crack his nut
on the mosaic tile

Sheehan the red-faced community cop
arrived in the nick of time
and the two Santas shared a sleigh
down the back road to Kilmainham.

Millennium Blitzkrieg
(Dublin's Millennium 1988)

It seemed as if the barracks were under siege,
spluttered gunfire fusillade
and Thor's heavy hammer shattering the dark,
bringing down the galaxies.

'A lot of young fools from the College'
boxed in at Richmond 'Estate'
Holes in the walls, more Moor Street manoeuvres,
history continuing off course?

Wellington, boot on the other foot ?
Joyce away from his ivory post !

Blitzkrieg waged over the Viceregal Lodge -
the parade ground, the military displays,
young Le Fanu watching the thunder clouds.

How bright the darkest spot, where Sturk,
where Cavendish and Burke, where lurks
the vile Mac Arthur.

Exploding ruby, lava emerald,
cool sapphire rippling scintilla:
Shirley, Californian, Himalayan blue,
Yellow horned, Oriental, Prickly-headed,
Corn, Flanders to Famine black.

Cascading coruscations, panicles of light
with each accelerated variegation,
burgeoning, blossoming, zooming us to worlds
of unfamiliar pleasures/ back again with no less wonder,
dreamlike, gently, safely down -
the third floor balcony of the four story block.

Life given the old City, the dead old City,
it's scattered remains, like Molly Malone's
waked in funereal night.

It was over when we noticed the surrounding kitchen
lights,
the finale faded with uncertain permanence,
but the sky bare, empty, unemployed.

The bombardment had missed Easter by only a week -
the movable feast, always evasive.

The poem is set in St Michael's Estate, formerly Richmond Barracks,
where the men of the Easter Rising were court martialled. Looking
towards the Phoenix Park from the balcony of my third floor flat I reflect
of the history of the area.

Ivory tower:: martello tower (one of a number, built at the same time as
Richmond Barracks as a lookout for Napoleon's ships), rented by Joyce.
Sturk: a character in Sheridan Le Fanu's *The House by The Churchyard*.
Mc Arthur: Malcome Mc Arthur, double murderer who was found
residing as a guest in the home of the Attorney General. Shirley,
Californian, Himalayan Blue, Yellow-horned, Oriental, Prickly-headed
and Corn are all types of poppy flowers, used here to describe the
various shapes and colours of the fireworks display.

Where All Friends Fear For You
An Ode To Michael Hartnett

in a hospital bed they revived you:
wide-hipped country nurses giving skip
to your romantic mischievous heart

and soon we saw you once again
shambling down Leeson Street
bowing to the passers by
or carrying a potted flower
for the girl in the bakers shop

such an oddity in the city
a squirrel from the woods
you were mugged on sight
your flat ransacked for a farmer's fortune
or the earnings of a poet

now at the Leeson Lounge, elbow on the bar
like Ledwidge heading off to war
you sail forth to that other place
where all friends fear for you

knowing you, you will return
with a chest of words -
still that familiar cigarette in hand -
wealth for all from your empty pockets
an old battered cap

In The Shade Of Francis Ledwidge

set in St. Michael's Estate,

I read you said that you were poor
and you had the wealth of royal Meath
a wealth of beauty in the land
its hills and fields and valley streams
red tongues of Pentecost - the whins
and the hawthorn with its *flag of truce*

and you were rich in company
with friends and loves and children
such as little Mary Halpin
who ran your errands from the village
Jackie Tiernan of the cows
and young Tommy Farrelly in Wilkinstown

at least you had Slane to return to
an escape from the city's *strife and din*
and Slane to occupy your mind
when forced to stay away; Slane to soar
above the smoke rising in clouds
as if from a huge censer shaken

All I have are remnants of the Barracks
and some of the vista you beheld
of the spire after spire of Dublin:
Daniel O'Connell's round tower...John's
Lane...St. Audeon's... the R.H.K...
the white monument to Wellington

my hills are high rise flats
I cannot even see the setting sun
the moon sustains me at night
and in the morning there is birdsong -
aye Frank, birdsong ! from the yew trees
and the headstones of Goldenbridge

but this is my domain, these my materials
the burnt out chassis of stolen cars
junkies pushers burglars and muggers,
the hard men and the hard women
and children -
children beautiful as children anywhere.

Evening in December

St. Michael's Estate 1999
on the eve of the Millennium

wagtails running
                across my path

beneath skyscape
of gold-red rippled cloud drift

and the whole set in aubergine

a common Godly spectacle
sent me thinking
                on things granted

4

Loss of my Parents

"In later years our roles were reversed"

The author with his mother on the balcony of 4, Ussher's Quay, overlooking the courtyard of the Brazen Head.

Under The Wheels

"Oh that was when we were living on the quays
there's a story about that, you know-
a story I could tell you
but it wouldn't be right
no, sure she's dead now, anyway
and it wouldn't be right -
no...no, it would not be right"

he forgets, he has already told me
and he will tell me again
again and again

"I often used to see her
by her stall at Michan's church
she was in her seventies then
and it was closer to her home.
There she would deal, entreat and bargain,
stick you with the 'old maid,' over ripe
Saturday morning market surplus
palmed to the bottom of the bag
beneath the ripe and the near ripe
selling for ten for the price of eight.
Her raucous Dublineese would fill my ears
and linger after me
the length of Church Street to Cleary's pub
where her evenings, and her earnings
were usually spent;
her little business folded, stowed.

I will always remember her quaint shoes
poking out from underneath the white apron
and the black hand-knitted shawl,
that was how I knew it was she that day
that was all I could make out
in-between the legs of the people in the crowd
who had gathered around.

There were voices
anxious, turning to despair
and an underlying murmur
as words bubbled at the mouths of the old folk present
and the murmur took:

It was 'her', wasn't it
who had first spotted the boy soldier
under the provisions lorry

and it was 'her', wasn't it, all those years ago
raised the alarm- "the poor child,
 he'll be crushed" -
in fear for his safety, she'd said,
 pointed him out
 perhaps without really thinking
- but then you never know.

Of course the 'Tans' led him off
and it wasn't long before the news
of how they'd tortured him,
flailed away his fingernails
thinking he would talk;

how he gave his life for liberty
one bitter Monday morning

-the songs, the ballads
that shamed their deeds -

*and **she***
she was the one who had given him away.

And was it odd
or was it somehow apt
that she was the one
whose headless corpse had come to rest
under the wheels"

"That was when we were living on the quays ....
poor miserable wretch
what a terrible way to end her life"

As a young boy my father witnessed the arrest of the patriot Kevin Barry in 1920, and later in life, as a married man, witnessed the death of the woman who was responsible for his capture. She had always protested her innocence, saying she had only done it because she had feared he would have been crushed when the van started. The event weighed heavily on her mind and some say she had a nervous breakdown, turning to drink for solace. She stumbled one day coming out of the pub and fell in the path of an on-coming car.

Gentle Crank

he had to get away
why? we never understood
all those times
when he would *disappear*
on the big occasions
like the typical party I remember
the house filled with old friends
the next door neighbours
and relatives I hardly knew
but no sign of himself
until much later
just as we had given up on him
when there was that familiar fumbling at the lock
several keys tried
before the jerk and rattle of the front door opening
the heavy tread up the stairs
followed by inaudibility
for a while
then the quiet descent
so quiet I'm sure he thought- noiseless
the gentle downward crank
        of the livingroom handle
the grand entrance
           the familiarity

out he had gone
to get out of our way, or
"To blow the stink off" himself,
 as he'd sometimes say
 making mother wince

anywhere would have done
but the nearest watering hole preferred
and there he must have sat
perhaps as cold as I
sipping a *frozen* pint
feeling quite alone
staring ahead
and seeing it all
sure it was just like being there
but somehow, you can cope better
at a distance

end of the pint
and there's only one place to go
back to where I never really left
back to be told
of all the things I have missed

Shells

                              on sunny days such as this
you never took us here
more likely to Malahide, Portmarnock
                              sometimes Sandymount

you loved the beach, and the water
were not beyond stripping off and getting in
while we lay on the sands and buried ourselves
- buried ourselves

looking up at the sun
you once spoke about the moon
how it revolved around the Earth
                              influencing the tides

how the Americans
would like to stick a flag in it
                    and how it would probably burst

later
when the sun went down
and the tide came in
you stood in shadow over us
                              come on now lads
                              time to go home
- time to go home

I leave you here
where sand is arid earth
where pebbles now are chippings dazzling white
and water by the bottle is borne from a tap

I hope you like the shells
I know you never had much time
                    for wishy-washy flowers

The After Thought

the curtain
closed
on the scene

silence
in place

of applause

time
to leave

as we made
our way
out through
the entrance
I paused

retraced
my steps

pulled back
the curtain
from around
the bed

rotten teeth
never to a dentist
in his life

but I moved my face
towards his...

remembered
it's the cheek

don't have to kiss
his lips...

I kissed his cheek
for all the years
boy and father
do not kiss...
did not kiss

and then...
I kissed his lips

Where He Has Got Himself

Alone, alone was not loneliness
but the waiting, the absurd anticipation
something to hold onto- rainbow hope
a gentle self delusion:

he had gone into town, was overdoing it
forgetting to come home, lost in some pub
-the Saturday routine
and she, left watching the clock
alert for his tread across the boards
"from the street to the toilet"

sitting to a solitary meal
she could still see a plate before her own
-his dinner drying up in the blue flame
dry, dry as the clay of Mount Jerome
lodged between the ridges of her shoes

Fading Images

I placed my hand upon my mother's head
and her wrinkled frame
a closing concertina shrank
in death

I broke down and my father put his arm around me
and I woke

it was 10 seconds before it hit me

mother is alive
father is dead

---

from a dream I had on the night of the day I was told that my mother
could have Alzheimer's disease

75

Carried Away

"a bucket of water
would sort them out"

mother said
referring to the couple
on the couch
in the movie we were watching

would she ?
I wondered, as I travelled back
to my wife
would my eighty three year old Mother
fill a bucket with water
someday when I'm not there
cast the contents over the television
blowing up the set
setting fire to the house
burning herself to death
leaving the neighbours
asking where her son was
when all this was going on

"And where were you"
asked my wife, on my return

Not Forgetting
The Backs Of My Ears

would she understand
the significance
of a book launch
the importance of having
someone special
present on the night
the publicity such an event
could generate?

"Mother" said I
my book will be launched
in Trim, County Meath
at the Wellington Court Hotel
and Noel Dempsey
Minister for the Environment
will launch the book"

"Oh," said she
with a twist of her jaw
then moving her dentures
into fourth gear
"You'll have to wash your face
for that"

My Mother Has Turned Into A Moth

she would never hurt hawk moths
even though they frightened her
she would always have me catch them
and release them to the garden

she's not thinking now of hawk moths
propped up here in Hospital 2
breathing what may be her last
wearing a mask for oxygen
connected at the nose by a long long tube

but I, trying not to dwell on or in the present
recall the touch of those ungainly creatures

    — wings beating in a flurry
      in the cup of my hands —

    and the loving mercy shown

Wings

the hospital is growing
growing growing

patient gone -

another bed

         up

    for

grabs

Bloomsday 2000

there were lots of blooms this Bloomsday
in mother's garden, every flower and rose,
the antirrhinums, even the poppies
                    showed their faces

flowers were sent *Interflora*
from Farmer Way, Parmelia,
Western Australia; Croydon,
close to the heart of London;
Midhurst, old world Sussex;

and people carried bouquets
from Inchicore, Ballyfermot, Clondalkin

cut and dying, yet still perfect
we laid them on the board
                    across her grave

5

Reflections

O And Bosnians

O to be a refugee
in Dublin
I'd be happy as a duck
in Stephen's green
weekly Government
hand-outs,
socialising money
and never
the suggestion
of work

but I was the O
in the O and Bosnian queue
at the labour exchange
and I the only one
called to heel
yea kneel
before the supervisor
-asked to beg
for a reprieve

no reasonable offer
could I refuse
even if the pay
were lower than the dole
and you know the medics
said my vertigo
was due to ... er...

idleness.

I cling to the spire
of John's Lane church
with a trowel
between my teeth
reminding myself
I'm *not* a racist
despite the efforts
of the State
to turn me into one
indeed I'm thinking
I would go to Bosnia
tomorrow

if I could return
as a refugee.

The Void Between Tick And Tock

The slow drip upon the lid of the pot
is the swinging platinum pendulum
of the clock in the house at Kickham Road
        Tick   Tock

Alex sitting by the black open hearth;
and Aunt Annie standing mute in shadow
her timid look so telling of her time
        Tick   Tock

    A seagull's cry startles me
    as it would have startled her
    in the quiet of her unease

Our hushed farewell: mother's words of solace
and Aunty's promise of an old fox fur
to Davy Crockett of the wayward hair
        Tick   Tock

With Alex still at the helm of his chair,
his head inclined to the old wireless set:
eavesdropping on the gossip of the world
        Tick   Tock

The slow slow drip upon the saucepan lid
is the swinging platinum pendulum
of the clock in the house at Kickham Road
        Tick   Tock

Dublin To A Dubliner

Dublin, to a Dubliner
       is like his loved one ageing:
in his eyes the image stays the same;
only at the Silver, at the Ruby,
at the Diamond is he forced to look;
and when with hurt, reality subsides
reliably the image is recalled
       to join him for another-
yet one more-
       throwback to sobriety.

Backstreets

where huddled youths at padlocked gates
throw down, pick up, I cut

as near to as the crow flies
across the northbank passing city folk
left in the lurch, in daylight shadowed
against walls, pre civil war walls

a woman with her baby breakfasting the smells
- hotel kitchen
winos reclined in communal slumber
shoed but stockingless

a forklift
            threatened
turned

another street, whiff of fish, decaying cabbage,
the reeking rich residuum of oranges,
cardboard boxes, cobbled ground
still the odd eye, dismal eyes that look, avert
try to ignore...

I seem like a king, I feel like a worm

Diceman

still forever

do they not sweep the streets before you
I used chuckle to myself
for often it seemed you walked in fear
of treading on broken glass

and gratefully I shared the wonder
of standing pedestrians
witnessing your snail's procession
through the main streets of Dublin

you were the Cheeky Prisoner,
rude Mona Lisa,
an awkward teapot on a crowded Dart
Dracula, scourge of Moore Street traders
or simply the Blonde Vamp

best of all, was when you just stood still
leaving us hanging for your pursed lips
wrinkled forehead, arched brows
any sudden movement

but it wasn't all fun
you worried us once in bloodied robes
your clown face weeping
for a suffering world

then your gaunt appearance
on the Late Late Show- apology to Mum;
your farewell wave in the Evening Herald;
the final procession to your resting place

McGinty, McGinty, your number's up -
you winked, oh! you *winked* at death
rather you had blinked.

Thom McGinty, in his role as the Diceman was Dublin's best loved
street character. He was also a brilliant mime artist. His upright walk,
unblinking stare and colourful costumes gave entertainment to tens of
thousands of people on his Grafton Street beat for almost 20 years. Even
during his illness, his love of life was awesome. He strived to create a
positive image of man living, not dying with Aids. Finally, he
succumbed to the disease in February, 1995.

Pat Egan's Soundcellar

it was usually the Stones
or Thin Lizzie
or Rory Gallagher
greeting me as I made my way
down the stair
into the ultra-violet sea of sound

to where Mr. Egan -
six foot in his stocking feet
except that you'd *never* see Pat
in his stocking feet -
would stand like a naval officer
manning a counter barely big
enough for him, a turntable
and a blue-jeaned long haired lady friend
who could stop you in your tracks

I'd hand across my old but pristine
records to be flipped between two index fingers
 while he'd frown at the sleeves
saying of the albums **bought in his store**
"You have obscure taste my friend
I cannot give you very much"

but stuck in a groove as I sometimes was
I'd settle for less than very much
and quit until another week

when rummaging through his bargain box
I'd hit upon the odd familiar record
marked
        'Rare
     Collectors Item'

and labelled with a price
that never failed to needle me.

Sandcastles

Wellington's memorial erection
by which young Dubliners pay homage
in the small hours

Napoleon's shrivelled penis
curio of collectors
divorced from god and man

and all along our coast, Martello towers

have tea while watching for the French
or see the Dubs led by Joyce
take on the Greeks

Baby Jane of Mary   dances
and saves souls
on the spot where the pillar stood

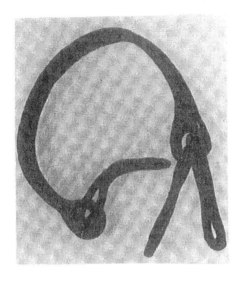

On 22nd. February 1982, The Evening Press carried the story of the discovery of an ancient slave collar found in the earth excavated at Wood Quay and deposited in a refuge dump near Inchicore. The article, penned by June Considine, ran to two full length pages under the banner headline **Island of Slaves and Collars**. It was my brother, Pat O'Meara, a numismatist and amateur archaeologist who made the find. He want on to uncover enough artefacts to host an exhibition at Dublin's Civic Museum. The Collar, a very rare example of the Irish slave trade and similar to types used in Britain, pre-Roman to 4th. Century AD, is now in the National Museum of Ireland. Although his work has featured in numerous books and magazines here and in Britain, he never received a finder's reward or even due recognition from the Museum. He now resides in Australia.

The Excavators

A variant soil, a clotted broth
-stewed wood, scallop
and scattered
black
     and gleaming oyster shell
among the stone, and cattle bone

a remnant from a bygone age
         a piece of china cup
contaminated in a world
      of used up cans of 7UP

and also in this earthen stack
a nail, a pin that drives me back:
bolts from longships
           broken pots,
blades of knives, implements,
polished eyes
      for fastening thread
   a coin in silver-   Ethelred

Unsettlers of unsettled peoples
settlements,
rivalling marauding antecedents
tore apart our treasured quay
   with arrogance, with J.C.B
destroyed the city's origins,
built great follies
         monuments
  that stand to their vulgarity.

These Ns and Ms of architecture
        alien, plain, pallid buildings
eclipse in shame the vista
                    of the neo-Gothic
and remain
                        ignored
undubbed by civic wit
so strong the public feeling
no nickname lovingly sticks.

To Inchicore, their excess borne
  in dumpers drippings
from the brim, the spew
            of old Dubh Linn

My boots are caked
                    centuries deep
the bray of machinery sounds
before me;
I track the tread to where
            earth eaters claim
the 'Spoil Heap'
  in furrow on the Liffey brow.

Le scavatrici

Un suolo variegato, un brodo denso
- legno frollato, conchiglia
e sparpagliato
nero
        e scintillante guscio d'ostrica
fra la pietra, e osso di bovino

lascito di tempo andato
        il pezzo di una tazza di porcellana
contaminato in un mondo
        di latte usate di 7UP

ed anche in questo cumulo di terra
 un chiodo, uno spillone mi riporta indietro:
bulloni di antichi navigli,
terraglie frantumate,
lame di coltello, arnesi,
crune levigate
            per fissare fili,
  moneta d'argento ... di Ethelred.

Disinsediatori di popoli disinsediati
insediamenti,
rivaleggianti saccheggianti antecedenti
han lacerato il nostro prezioso approdo
            con arroganza, con i JCB,
distrutto le origini della città,
eretto follie immense-
                        monumenti
che stanno a testimoni della loro volgarità

Queste architetture a N, a M,
alieni, banali pallidi edifici
eclissano a dileggio la vista
   del Neo- Gotico
 e restano
     ignorati
senza nomi conferiti dalla civica arguzia
tanto forte è la pubblica avversione
che neppure
 un affettuoso soprannome gli s'attacca.

A Inchicore l'eccesso è trasportato
in autcarri gocciolanti
dai bordi, il rigurgito
   della vecchia Dubh Linn.

I miei stivali sono immersi
   in secoli di fango
-davanti a me
risuona il raglio delle macchine;
io seguo le tracce fino a dove
I mangia-terra reclamano
     "ricche spoglie"
lasciando solchi sulla fronte del Liffey.

Translated by Giuseppe Serpillo
Dr. of Anglo-Irish Literature
University of Sassari, Italy.

The Brazen Head

at the Brazen Head
once a meeting place of patriots

yuppies and tourists stand over pints
blocking drinkers from the bar

The 'Brazen Head,' as I remember it; before the lane-way
to the entrance and the adjoining shops were demolished.

The Author

Liam O'Meara is founder of Syllables Writers' Group and chairman of the Francis Ledwidge Society. In 1993, he collaborated with Karl Judge on an experimental work of poems and drawings titled *Guardians of the Poem*. In 1997, he edited *Francis Ledwidge, The Poems Complete* and in 1999, followed with a biography titled, *A Lantern On The Wave*. Liam has won numerous poetry awards, including most recently: Premio Città di Olbia (Italy) prize 2001, The Gerard Manley Hopkins, The Tipperary Arts prize, Riposte readers choice, and a diploma- his sixth from the Robert Burns Club, (Scotland) His letters appear regularly in national and provincial newspapers. The Sunday Tribune awarded him a holiday prize for letter of the week while another letter with a poem was broadcast on RTE Radio's 'What it says in the Papers.' Other broadcasts have included radio interviews with John Bowman and a feature spot on RTE Television's 'Cúrsaí Ealaíne'. Most notable recent live performances were, Jury's Hotel- Poetry Ireland's tribute night to the late Michael Hartnett, a guest appearance with singing group ANUNA- Christmas '97, and Wexford Arts Festival 2000. On 3rd. May 2001, Liam addressed the Ireland Institute with a lecture on Thomas Mac Donagh, Francis Ledwidge and the 1916 Rebellion.